Science All Around Me

Hot and Cold

Heinemann
LIBRARY

Karen Bryant-Mole

First published in Great Britain by Heinemann Library, Halley Court, Jordan Hill, Oxford OX2 8EJ
a division of Reed Educational & Professional Publishing Ltd.

OXFORD FLORENCE PRAGUE MADRID ATHENS MELBOURNE AUCKLAND KUALA LUMPUR
SINGAPORE TOKYO IBADAN NAIROBI KAMPALA JOHANNESBURG GABORONE PORTSMOUTH
NH (USA) CHICAGO MEXICO CITY SAO PAULO

Designed by Jean Wheeler
Commissioned photography by Zul Mukhida
Consultant – Hazel Grice
Printed in Hong Kong / China

02 01 00 99 98
10 9 8 7 6 5 4 3 2 1

ISBN 0 431 07830 0

British Library Cataloguing in Publication Data

Bryant-Mole, Karen
   Hot and cold. - (Science all around me)
   1. Temperature - Juvenile literature 2. Thermodynamics - Juvenile literature
   I. Title
   536.5

A number of questions are posed in this book. They are designed
to consolidate children's understanding by encouraging further
exploration of the science in their everyday lives.

Words that appear in the text in bold can
be found in the glossary.

Acknowledgements
The Publishers would like to thank the following for permission to reproduce photographs: Eye Ubiquitous 20; James Davis 12; Positive
Images 6; Tony Stone Images 10, 18 (Lori Adamski Peek), 14 (Joel Bennett), 16 (Michael Rosenfeld), 22 (John and Eliza Forder), Zefa 4.

Every effort had been made to contact copyright holders of any material reproduced in this book. Any omissions will be
rectified in subsequent printings if notice is given to the Publisher.

Contents

Temperature

'Hot' and 'cold' are words that are used to describe **temperature**.

The food that this waiter is carrying on his tray is cold.

? *Can you think of a food that is usually served hot?*

See for yourself ...

Holly is eating her favourite meal. She is having pizza, followed by strawberries and cream.

The pizza is hot but the strawberries and cream are cold. Is your favourite food hot or cold?

Temperature words

There are lots of words to describe **temperature**.

The water in this swimming pool could be described as warm. Other temperature words include cool, **tepid** and **lukewarm**.

Do you prefer swimming in warm water or cool water?

See for yourself ...

Emerich and Jonathan are washing up.

Emerich thinks the water is warm but Jonathan thinks it is lukewarm.

Words like 'hot', 'warm' and 'lukewarm' are useful but they don't tell us the exact temperature

Measuring temperature

To find out exactly how hot or cold something is, we have to **measure** its **temperature**.

Temperature is measured using a **thermometer**. A thermometer is being used to measure this girl's body temperature.

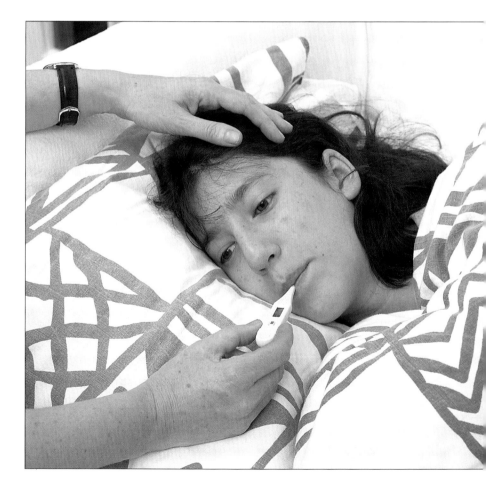

Temperature is measured in degrees.

See for yourself ...

Jessica is using a room
thermometer to measure
the temperature of the air.

If the air temperature gets
hotter, the red liquid
inside the thermometer
rises up.

The number next
to the top of the
liquid shows Jessica
the air temperature.

9

Feeling temperature

We feel **temperature** through our skin.

The people in this picture are sitting in the sunshine.
They can feel the hot sun through the skin on their faces,
arms and legs.

(i) *When you eat, you feel the temperature of
the food through the skin inside your mouth.*

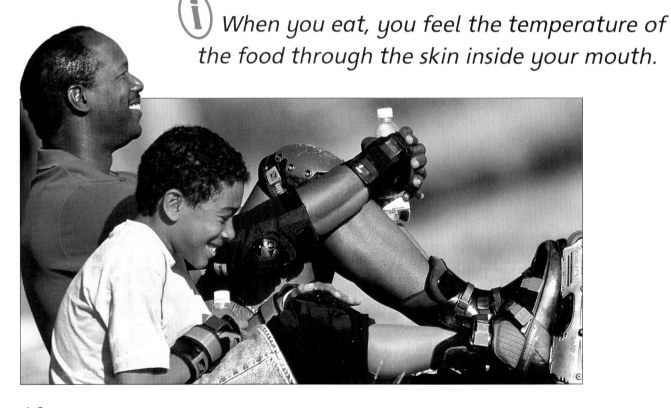

See for yourself ...

Emerich asked his mum to fill
one bowl with warm water
and another with cold water.

Emerich can't tell them
apart just by looking.
But as soon as he
tests the water
with his finger,
he can feel which
is which.

Weather

Weather can feel hot or cold.

In winter, the air is colder than it is in summer. The cold air makes us feel cold. The hot air in summer makes us feel hot.

Which season do you prefer, summer or winter?

See for yourself ...

We wear different types of clothes in the winter and the summer.

One of these children is wearing winter clothes. The other is wearing summer clothes.

Can you tell which is which?

Freezing

If **liquids** get cold enough, they will **freeze**.

This iceberg is made of frozen water. Ice cubes and hail stones are made of frozen water, too.

(i) *The **temperature** at which something freezes is called its freezing point.*

See for yourself ...

Holly wants to freeze some orange juice, to make an ice lolly.

She is pouring the juice into a clean, plastic pot. She has pushed a clean lolly stick through the lid.

When she has put the lid on the pot, her dad will freeze it in the freezer.

Melting

Heating things can make them **melt**.

The metal in this picture has been heated in a very hot fire called a furnace. It is now so hot that it has melted and can be poured.

 *Things that have melted are described as 'molten'.*

See for yourself ...

Jessica put some chocolate on a saucer.

She placed the saucer on a windowsill, where the sun shone onto it.

After a while she went back to the saucer.

The chocolate had started to melt in the heat.

Changing air temperature

The **temperature** of something can be changed by the temperature of the air around it.

When the air around this snowman starts to warm up, the snow will turn to water. The snowman will begin to **melt**.

(i) *Snow is made of tiny pieces of frozen water.*

See for yourself ...

Jonathan's soup was too hot for him to drink and so he left it for a while.

The colder air around the soup soon cooled the soup down.

Now its temperature is just right!

Cooking

Heat can be used to cook food.

There are lots of different ways to heat food.

It can be boiled in water or fried in oil. It can be baked in the oven or grilled. It can be microwaved or even barbecued.

? *How is your favourite meal cooked?*

See for yourself ...

Alex is eating a potato.
It has been baked in the oven.

Potatoes can be cooked in
many ways. How many
different ways can you
think of?

Changes

This chef is making some bread. He is going to bake the **dough** in the oven.

Heat changes the dough from a squashy, stretchy **mixture** into a **solid** loaf of bread.

ⓘ *When it has been heated, the bread cannot be changed back into squashy dough.*

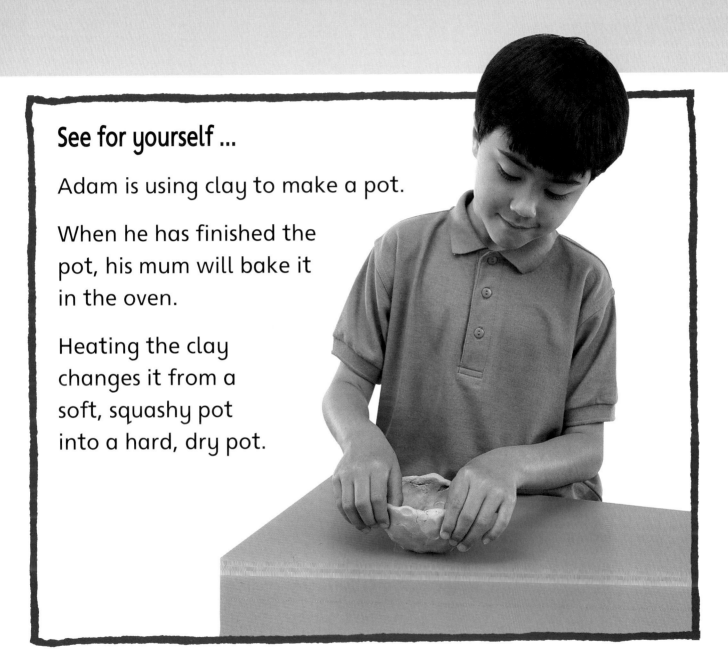

See for yourself ...

Adam is using clay to make a pot.

When he has finished the
pot, his mum will bake it
in the oven.

Heating the clay
changes it from a
soft, squashy pot
into a hard, dry pot.

Glossary

degrees the units or 'steps' that are used to measure temperature

freeze make something so cold that it turns into a solid

heating making hotter

liquid something that can be poured

lukewarm cooler than warm but warmer than cool

measure find the amount of something

melt become liquid

mixture anything made by mixing things together

solid something with a shape that stays the same

temperature the heat of something

tepid similar to lukewarm

thermometer an object used to measure temperature

Index